Featuring the Human Race Club

You Can BE A WINNER!

Written by Joy Berry

Illustrated by Bartholomew

GROLIER ENTERPRISES CORP.

Executive Producer: Ron Berry
Producer: Marilyn Berry
Editor: Kate Dickey
Consultants: Dr. David Braff and Associates,
Kathy McBride, and Ellen Klarberg
Design and Production: Abigail Johnston
Typesetting: Curt Chelin

4

If you want to be happy and healthy, you need to achieve something. You need to get something done.

There will always be goals that you will **need** and **want** to achieve.

Whenever you achieve something **YOU WIN!**

Some of your achievements may be more difficult than others. Some may require you to make more effort. The more effort you make, the more you will enjoy winning.

You can be a winner if you **set yourself up to win!**

First you must decide what you want to achieve.

Be realistic when you are deciding what to do.

Find out exactly what it will take. Research the subject.

- Read
- Observe
- Experiment
- Talk to other people

Make sure that you are **physically** able to do what you want to do.

Consider your
- age
- body size
- body shape
- physical coordination and ability

Make sure that you are **mentally** able to do what you want to do.

Consider your
- interests (those subjects about which you are naturally curious)
- mental abilities

Make sure the **conditions** are right for you to do
what you want to do.

Consider

- **where** you live, work, and go to school. (Is there a place nearby where you can do what you need to do?)
- the **people** who surround you. (Are there people around who can help you?)
- the **resources** that are available to you. (Do you have access to the things you will need?)
- the **time** involved. (Do you have enough time to do what you need to do?)

Once you have decided what you want to achieve,
you need to **develop a plan of action.**

Do this by making a list of every task you need
to do.

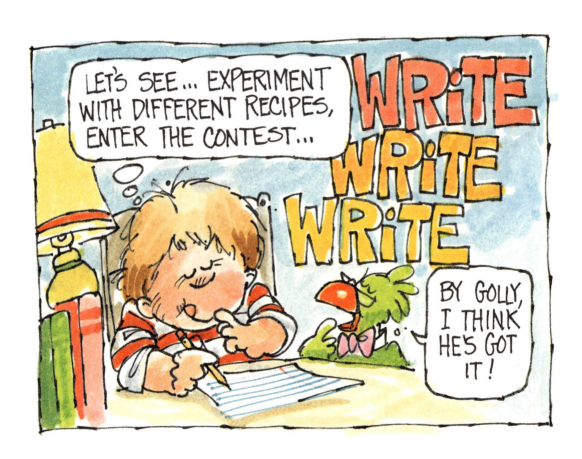

Next, organize your list. Put the tasks in the order in which they must be completed. Do this by determining what you need to do first, second, third, and so on.

You have set yourself up to win when you have
• realistically decided what to do
• developed a plan of action

Now you are ready to **be a winner!**

There are **six rules** that winners follow in order to win.

Rule # 1

WINNERS Think GOOD THOUGHTS.

They think positive thoughts about themselves
and what they are doing.

Your mind is extremely powerful. It controls
everything you do. If it tells you to do good
things, you will most likely do good things.
If it tells you to fail, you will most likely fail.
It is important for you to think positive thoughts.
It is also important for you to avoid negative
thoughts.

RULE #2
WINNERS FOCUS ON THEIR GOAL.

They think about the positive outcome of their efforts rather than the work and risk involved.

If you think about everything you need to do to win, you may feel overwhelmed and want to give up. If you think about losing, you may become discouraged and stop trying. But if you think about winning, you will be inspired. Everything you need to do will be less difficult and you will want to keep trying.

This is why you need to focus on your goals.

29

Rule #3

WiNNERS keep THEiR WORD.

They do what they say they will do. They keep the promises they make to others and, more importantly, they keep the promises they make to themselves.

If you want to keep your word, you must not **procrastinate** or **escape**. Procrastination is putting off what needs to be done. Escaping is trying to avoid doing a task by doing something else. These things can prevent you from keeping your word. When you have promised to do something, it is important that you do it as soon as you can.

RuLe # 4
WINNeRS Take ADVANTaGe oF CoMPeTiTioN.

Competition is getting involved with other people for the purpose of winning. Winners use competition in a positive rather than negative way.

The Positive Side of Competition

Competition can give you an opportunity to **learn** what you should and should not do. It enables you to watch other people. As you see them making mistakes, you can learn to avoid those mistakes. As you see them succeeding, you can learn what you need to do to succeed.

Competition can make you want to **improve**. It allows you to compare your efforts with the efforts of others. Seeing what other people have achieved may encourage you to do as well, or even better.

Competition can encourage you to **try** because it shows you what is possible.

When you see someone do something, you learn that it can be done. You may be more willing to try if you know that something can be done.

This is important because you cannot win if you do not try.

The Negative Side of Competition

Competition can **distract** you. If you want to win, you must pay attention to what you are doing. You cannot do this if you are spending your time and energy watching other people. It is important for you to concentrate on **your** efforts, rather than on the efforts of others.

Competition can **discourage** you. Focusing on the accomplishments of other people may cause you to feel inferior. You may begin to think that you cannot do as well as they can. You may become discouraged and stop trying. If you want to win you must remain confident and hopeful so you will not give up.

Competition can **limit** you. Focusing on the achievements of others may cause you to think that what they are doing is all that can be done. You may have the potential to do something that no other person has thought of doing. You must not limit yourself to the accomplishments of other people. Instead, you need to be creative and decide for yourself what you are going to do.

Competition can be used to **dominate and control others.** Some people compete to prove they are better than other people. They want to be considered better so they can dominate and control others. They want to be in control because they want to have their way all of the time. This is unfair and can cause many problems. You must be sure you do not compete in order to dominate and control others.

RULE #5
WiNNeRS Take ADVaNTaGE oF SETBACKS.

A setback happens when something goes wrong. A winner turns a setback into something positive.

When things go wrong you are usually forced to stop what you are doing for a while. **You can use this time to your advantage.** Think about what you are doing. Re-evaluate your efforts. You may discover that it would be better if you were doing something differently.

41

When you find that you need to do something differently, **revise your plan.** Your new plan will most likely be better than your old one. This will make you want to try harder and will increase your chances of winning.

It is important that you do not focus on a setback.
It is also important that you **do not become
discouraged and give up.** It may help if you
remember that setbacks are bound to occur
because people cannot always control everything
that happens to them. People who try to
accomplish something have one or more setbacks.
It would be better for you to spend your time and
energy making your new plan work.

Rule # 6
Winners take Advantage of Failure.

A winner turns a failure into something positive.

Failure can give you an opportunity to learn what
you should and should not do. If you fail because
you did something wrong, you can learn to avoid
doing the same thing again. If you fail because you
neglected to do something, you can learn to do it
the next time.

45

You can learn from your failures if you react to them appropriately. You must not focus on them This will only make you feel bad. Instead you must focus on the lessons to be learned.

You must not be impatient with yourself when you fail. This will only make you feel as though you cannot do anything right. When you feel this way, you will not be able to do your best. If you do not do your best, you may not be able to win.

It may help you to remember that everyone fails at one time or another. Failure seems to be something that every person must go through in order to win.

When you...
- realistically decide what to do
- develop a plan of action
- think good thoughts
- focus on your goal
- keep your word
- take advantage of competition
- take advantage of setbacks
- take advantage of failure

...you can **BE A WINNER!**